Short Sleepwalkers

Jeremy Bell

Published 2017
Caliburn Publishing
Irsha Street
Appledore
Devon
e-mail: jeremybellvisions@gmail.com
website www.poeticfire.co.uk

Cover idea - Jeremy Bell –

Cover artist – Daniel Bell

ISBN-13: 978-1548832896
ISBN-10: 1548832898

Shouting at Sleepwalkers
Jeremy Bell

Other books by Jeremy Bell

Contents

Songs

FOREWORD
- Shouting at Sleepwalkers –

A book of rhythmic verse, prose and satirical song

Every age can be said to be unique – but ours is truly unique, because for the first time in human history we are being faced with the reality that there are 'limits to growth', and that our human impact on the natural world upon which we are entirely dependent, is unsustainable.

If you don't agree, then consider the following –

Take a physical map of the planet printed circa 1850 and compare it to one printed circa 2000. Compare the areas of forest and jungle, desert, and the land area now covered by towns and cities. Compare the global populations. In 1850 there were about 1.2 billion people living on the planet compared to over 7.2 billion today. Then consider the biocide of flora and fauna – birds, fish, bees and other pollinators, as well as the widespread slaughter of elephant and rhino etc. Hold in mind the plastic-laden seas and other deadly wastes we are still dumping in them, and the deadly particulates filling the air of urban centres – not to mention the inexorable increase in the amount of carbon dioxide we are pumping into the atmosphere, as well as methane from the melting tundra.

It was nearly 30 years ago that the front cover of The Times Weekend Magazine showed a picture of a felled forest with the caption – 'THE PLANET IS DYING – WHAT ARE YOU GOING TO DO ABOUT IT?' Very little it seems, as the drive for ever increasing production and consumption continues apace at the expense of the planet, and politicians of both left and right still believe that economic growth is not only possible, but absolutely essential.

We are cutting off the branch on which we are all sitting, and every year the Spring is becoming ever more silent.

We might also ask ourselves why, as the richest most prosperous generation that has ever existed so widely on the globe, we are not happier than our grandparents' generation? Why, with the World Wide Web of the global communications industry, is loneliness now so prevalent, and a principle cause of mental illness, and religious fundamentalism and fascism is now attracting so many 'rational' and 'educated' people to their banners?

Yet never have we had such opportunities to open our minds and hearts to the amazing revelations of science that are shedding so much light upon the nature of reality and how our universe operates.

So how are today's poets responding to the above? What are they saying about these things?

The best poetry calls out from the depths of the human condition re-expressing the timeless shaping forces of archetype, symbol and myth evoking the suffering, joy and beauty of existence in all of it's contradictions, challenging every new generation to see life anew. Think of the First World War Poets, and earlier ones such as Wordsworth, whose use of rhyme and heart-felt reasoning connects body and soul, while reflecting on the growing schizoid experience of industrial man as he started to divorce himself from the natural rhythms of nature. As he wrote -

'Our meddling intellects

Misshape the beauteous forms of things

We murder to dissect.' (Expostulation and Reply)

Why is it that the discipline of rhyme, which helps internalise and capture meaning, is often so disdained today? Is it because any attempt to express deeper meaning and vision has been eclipsed by ephemeral feeling, and thus, much modern poetry loses any prophetic voice, and is seen by the majority of people as being exclusively high-brow or at best, a marginal art form?
I believe Henry Miller's cutting commentary on the state of modern

poetry, is a challenge to all who would aspire to that high office. In his study of Rimbaud – The Time of the Assassins, he writes -

'Our poets today are jealous of the name but show no disposition to accept the responsibility of their office. They have not proved themselves poets;

They are content to call themselves such. They are writing not for a world that hangs on their every word but for one another. They justify their impotence by deliberately making themselves unintelligible. They are locked in their glorified little egos; they hold themselves aloof from the world for fear of being shattered at the first contact. They are not even personal, when one gets right down to it, for if they were we might understand their torment and delirium such as it is. They have made themselves as abstract as the problems of the physicist. Theirs is a womb-like yearning for a world of pure poetry in which the effort to communicate is reduced to zero.'

I have striven to write poetry, but over the years, slowly realised what a high calling this is; thus, I now class myself more as a versifier.

Nevertheless, what you will read in this book is my attempt to engage with the realities of life – living now as we all do, on the edge of time. The writings, which are shaped by my own idiosyncratic nature and existential desperation, are my attempt to at least try and understand something of what my short life means in relation to the banality of much of modern culture, and it's detrimental effect on both people and nature - as well as my own search for spiritual depth – but also the wonders of scientific discovery which can, with imagination re-open the 'doors of perception,' and re-awaken those who seek the deep truths taught by the world's great spiritual teachers.

Jeremy Bell 2017

TRANSCENDING PRESENCE

This so solid sphere
Is but a light- kiss away
From other dimensions

This heavy, hurting hardness
And silky, soggy softness
Numb nudity of winter
And bursting heart of spring

These mad desires of being
And arousing scents of feeling
The bruising bass of fury
Pure voice on angel wing

Sunrise for the seeing
Sunset for the blinding
And all the shades of dying
In three dimensions cling

As beams of the eternal
From the holographic kernel
Seep through this clinging matter
To display upon the platter
A richer feast of plenty
And a grail that's never empty

While the fisherman forsaken
Bids the sleeping guest awaken
And consume the offering.

SACRED OPENING

When the arc consumes
The wine in the cup
The bread on the platter
Then the Royal Arch
Opens up it's sealed doors
And the temple curtain
Is torn aside
And through that holy gap
Streams another fire
A timeless resonation
Through this dense excruded gravitation
This outlaw – rogue dimension.

IN THE DANCE TO BECOMING

Every wave of light and sound
Dances through the wakening ground
Creates a violin than a bow
To manifest the music's flow

Alienated in a dream
Of frozen matter's desperate scream
Fighting for each empty gain
In vain attempt to break the chain

Of sense linked to external form
That analyses every dawn –
Like trying to pin down the dance
Of butterflies around a lance

This patriarchal paradigm
Worshipping a god of time
This ego fight to rule the three
Dimensions of it's agony

Can never cauterise the flow
Of energy that moves the bow.
Inside this hologram of now
We only breathe the why and how.

Each apart and each a whole
A verse sung in an opening scroll
Of star and photon, soul and seed
In live dimensions of it's need.

HOMO-IGNORAMUS

The animals held a summit
Linked telepathically
A crisis meeting to discuss
'Humankind – the Enemy'.
Beneath an old acacia tree
Chairman lion gave a growl;
'Homo-ignoramus's rule
Threatens every fish and fowl,
Free-ranging and farmed quadrupeds
And the poor of their own kind;
There are three options I can see
To cure man's ravening mind.
We could unite and kill them all
And betray their misplaced trust;
Pretend we're all as mad as them
Help them turn the earth to dust;
Or a tenth of every species
Could select an awesome day
And fearlessly destroy themselves –
It's just possible they may
Wake up, take stock of what they've done
And repent their stupid pride
And come and make their peace with us
For the sake of those who died'.

His low growl ceased, he sniffed the wind
Reading his listener's mind – then
Heard the caw of a wise jackdaw –
'I'm not sure I can find
Too much logic in these options,
But I think there is a fourth –
The most exploitive of humanity
Seem to all live in the north.

I suggest a mass migration
To the Southern Hemisphere,
Let the poor and starving eat us
Show we animals still care.
Their silent skies and empty fields
Will reveal our sacrifice;
The survival of creation
May be worth this heavy price'.

A dread quiet filled the tele-sphere
As each animal took stock
Of their terrible position
Twixt a hard place and a rock.
But then upon the solemn air
Was heard the strangest ringing
Massed choirs of bacteria
And viruses were singing.

'A billion, billion of us bugs
Live on every human skin,
Inside his every orifice,
We're his nearest kith and kin.
We, the lowliest life of all
Have no enemy or friend,
Yet, we the lords of man's proud life
Have already planned his end.
His sterile purposes are vain
Before our mutating power,
The more unnatural he becomes
Quicker draws his dying hour.'

And this is why all creatures stare
At homo-ignoramus;
The rabid ruler of the earth
Is fatally contagious.

THE END OF NATURE

The dark is no longer natural
Sodium lights now taunt the stars
Starving it of mystery.

The daylight is no longer natural
We have rent the heavens
And the sun glares at us.

The sky is no longer natural
Sunsets are glazed with chemical colourings
Smouldering in the burnished blue.

The wind is no longer natural
It blows from man-made deserts,
Burning forests and concrete cities
The dust and dioxides of human excrement.

The rain is no longer natural
Diluted with additives
It is now powerless
To baptise my daughter's hair.

The rivers and streams are no longer natural
They flow sterile clear
Running like athletes on steroids.

The subtle symphony of nature can no longer be heard
Except in snatches – in desert places.
The tinnitus of traffic drowns the choral of the lark.

My children will never find that space
That unmapped, pristine place
Of the untrammelled wild
Where I walked as a child.

GREEN BELT SACRIFICE

Cllr Blather and Cllr Stern
And a builder named Cllr Hod
Were viewing some green belt round their town
And thinking it rather odd
That all the animals, plants and trees
Walkers and dogs and birds and bees –
And none to be seen with a frown.
'They're enjoying themselves', growled Cllr Blather
'Playing not working', snarled Cllr Stern
'I'd cover it in houses' said Cllr Hod.

'I've a developer friend' said Cllr Hod
'Who will pay a good price for the lot
The Chief Execs in need of a penny
To add to his pension pot
And, as Chair of Planning, Cllr Blather,
I'm sure between us we could gather
A voting majority'
'This town must grow', growled Cllr Blather
'We've got to compete', snarled Cllr Stern
'We'll each trouser a packet', crowed Cllr Hod.

When the Planning Committee met to decide
Whether to build on the land
Hundreds e-mailed and hundreds wrote
Determined to take a stand
And fight for their right to enjoy this space
And give the Council a kick in the face
And threaten them with their vote.
'The young need housing', burbled Cllr Blather
'And housing means jobs', snarled Cllr Stern
'You can't halt progress', said Cllr Hod

An objector said 'This land was bequeathed
To the people for recreation'.
But another replied, 'the deeds have been lost
Under council re-organisation'.
'These woods may provide a rare habitat
For a natter jack toad or a long-eared bat
But to prove it will certainly cost'.
'They hold all the cards', a small man spat
'We've got to keep trying', squeaked a Green Party girl
'This is Britain, they'll listen', quoth a prat.

The sun crept away from the fields and woods
Ashamed it had witnessed this scene.
A dog walker halted, shuddered – then ran
At the sight of the rope through the green
And the boy that hung from the end of the line
With eyes like grapes on a ripened vine.
'Whose child hangs here by the bank of the burn?'
'And who's his father?' they asked in dread
'It's the only son of Cllr Stern.'

'Dad, please listen, please try and see
Publish this letter, let everyone know
And think of the reason I've done this –
Then this seed I have planted, may grow.
The arms of this oak held me and my den
That I built in it's boughs when I was just ten
This is one of the friends I shall miss
And my woods, my stream and the way that it weaves
The songs of the robins, thrushes and larks
And the dance of the light through the leaves.'

'This place is special, Dad, not just to me
But to hundreds of others who weighed down with care

Come to this place just to walk, think or sit
And be fed by the life that lives here.
The primroses, bluebells, blackberries, sloes
Hazel-nuts, squirrels, badgers and crows
Each and everyone holds this place dear.
But the threat to this land is little compared
To what's happening all over the world
And that is what makes me so scared.'

'This wood is my rainforest – don't cut it down
The Amazon, like this my small stream,
But they're often used as sewers and drains
So there's far fewer fish to be seen
And far fewer whales, rhino and bear -
My woodpecker left this time last year
It's all like a horrible dream.
We'll starve if we wipe out the insect and bee
We need these animals, fishes and plants
Dad, they're part of yourself and of me.'

Your son
Christopher Stern

THE PROPHESYING WIND

Will you not listen
To the hysterical wind,
The unchained, rebel lunatic
Screaming the agonies
Of the dumb
Cowering in the chain-sawed wilderness,
Galeing at the suicidal empire
Of tarmac and concrete
That drips its alien compounds
Into the aquifers
Of the struggling earth?
She smells of the stinking skins of beasts,
Locusts and mosquitoes are her portents
For the white, sterilised suckers
Screening their lives away
In self-locking cages,
Climatically controlled,
Filtering their own pollution
And untamed fears.

Burn, burn the goddess Gaia;
Though her wild innards
Are but half understood.
Even when dissected,
Re-constitute her genes
In your own defaced image.
For your feet –
Too sensitive for suffering
But cruel enough to trample,
Have become leperous
Stumbling over her prostrate carcass

As you –

Lust mournfully over the kill,
This death – your death
Of untried lives,
This death that need not be.

THE PRESENCE OF JOY

I dive through the waves bum-naked
And roar with the incoming tide
Praise and dance round my fire of driftwood
Gasp at your thighs open wide.

Mid the scents of the gorse and the heather
And the skylark calling it's mate
I sing as my sap surges upwards
Melt any winter of hate.

For this is the moment of living
Once again we're a girl and a boy
Gone are the past and the future
This is the presence of joy.

EMERGING LOVE-LIGHT

Truth is drawn up from the springs
Of the ground of being
The silent reassurance
That all will be well
That all will make sense.
It exposes it's pictures
In the darkroom of the soul
Healing the shapes of nightmares
And lovingly breathing
Every fear away.

THE JOY OF THE PRESENT TENSE

Grandparents, two grandchildren
The latter skipping, the former stiffening
But not as solidly ageless as the cliffs,
Battered, weathered, gouged and mined.
They are the stage for these two brief generations
Who now look out over the sleeping sea
Nuzzling the towering, ravaged ramparts.
Their dog sniffs, the girl points
Her brother waves
At the gliding gulls.
The grandparents ponder decaying erections,
Those solid wheel houses
Beneath which sweat and straining muscle
Picked and tunnelled
Expending it's ore–lust
In a mere 200-year old orgasm.
Now these ravaged ruins are romanticised,
Weathering more slowly than the grandparents,
But not as slowly as the ageless granite
Glinting in the last sun-spill from the sea
While the tender children laugh and skip
Unconscious of eternal bruising.

EMPTY GRAIL

Who hears the heart – scream
Tearing the womb?
Only the green-child
Fronding the earth.

Who sees the blood?
Not ticket-people,
Blind watchers,
Time-tourists.

Who reaches to touch
Across the divide
In the night of the soul
The spasms of nerves?

Who licks the sores,
The tears of the wounds?
Only the dogs,
The loyal dumb.

Who smells the death?
Only the hungry
Burying their blood
In flint-fields of hope.

Who did not ask?
'Why this dripping lance?
Why this loving cup?
Whom does it serve?'

Shall Klingsor be king
By the 'Monsanto Matter'
Poisoning the Grail
Exhausting the platter?

Dust-bowls of hearts cry
Along the web of one brain:
Gone the Shekinah
Driven from Logres again.

DISTOPIA

When the tortured silence
Is heard again,
After the bombast:
When man's mechanised dream
Lies dumb – rust-rotting
Only the rhythmic hum
Of the struggling organism
Will still be making music –
Ravaged, faltering notes
Striving for harmonies.
Then wounded, traumatised man
Will curse his ancestors,
Outlaw any hint of lost, Atlantean power,
Worship every uncertain element
Displayed by nature,
Project his every fear
On to all that sings of something higher,
Deeper, transcendent, omnipresent –
Until the weeping, dribbling spring
Begins to rise again
Cleansing the toxins
From land and mind.
Then earth, fire, air and water
Flora and fauna
Will reach out again in friendship
Bidding the survivors
To join the healing dance,
Lead them again
In concert.

EARTH, AIR, WATER, FIRE – PLUS

From a frequency scarce heard
Breathes the sound of love's pure word
A timeless kingdom's open door
Bathing every time-bound pore
And these four elements at war.

Blood-soaked earth
Scream-torn air
Tear-filled seas
Consuming fire.

IF THE PRIEST SPOKE

Curse this cross that nails my mind
Confines me in this tortured cell
Naked, but for one wrapped towel
Around the sex I'm taught is hell.

These polarised, magnetic spikes
This rack that stretches every joint –
Is this a resurrection life
Or what I worship, but a point

Towards a mirage in the sand
Where virgins wait to drain my powers?
Is my vain worship in-between
The aching thighs of time's twin towers?

Oh, I could wish a madman's plane
Could lunge inside, expunge each tower
Destroying both to end God's blame
And let my soul burn in that fire.

THE PRIEST REPLIES

Hold me in the healing hour
Touch my self-inflicted bruise
I am terrified of love
You draw me on, but I abuse.

All the resurrecting loving
All the mysteries unfolding
All the hungry, urgent calling
That lights the knowledge I've been trawling.

Can I worship you as Love?
Yes, you are my most trusted friend
You walk with me along life's path
And light my way, and light my end.

THE SECULAR MAN SPEAKS

Now hanging above the earth
Mindful only of a swirl of images
And spiritual drought
I have become dis-eased
Conscious of my acidic, bill-filled stomach
Car seat body, screen-screwed eyes
Tense, twittering neurons
In semi-sleepless nights.
This aging body needs Viagra,
The regular pump of a gym treadmill
A bronzing holiday or big lottery saviour.

I saw a hearse today
And wondered about the empty husk –
Those suited remains within that polished box
With it's gilded handles
Transported in a black-bright limousine
Adorned with dying flowers
To an industrial burning centre.
What do I live for?
To whom do I give my allegiance?
Where and when did I lose
My child's heart's vision?
How much have I really loved?

SCREENED OUT

Why do you ignore the rest of creation?
Are you now so deaf – blind and dumb
To be no longer aware
Of that great orchestra of birdsong,
Those muting choirs still singing in every tree and hedgerow
That can lift your spirit to the skies?

Are you deaf to the snuffling hedgehog
Don't you look for the sleek water rat
Or the owl as it swoops in the moonlight
The butterfly, mole or the bat?

The vole, the badger and slow worm
The fox trotting back in the dawn –
When did you last see a dragonfly
Or delight in the spread of frogspawn?

When did you last run barefoot
Through a meadow of web-dewed grass
Or lie down in clusters of wild flowers
So still, that a deer wandered past?

When did you last gather blackberries
Hazel-nuts, crab apples, sloes
Rose hips, mushrooms and king-cups
Inhale those scents through your nose?

Are you scared of the silence inside you
Do you only see light through a screen
Divorced from the planet around you
And all that is rampant and green?

Your i-pad and mobile have dumbed you
Numbed the spirit that bids you engage
With all of the rest of your nature
Your free-range – don't live in a cage.

OLD

The warmth doesn't seem as warm as it was
And the cold's like a wintering tide
But I remember long summer spells
When muscle-taut skin glowed with pride.
Though the winters were sharp as icicles' spikes
That pierced every bone to the marrow,
I grew in it's grip, and drained every drip
Thirsty and eager and callow – but
Now my old body can't capture the warmth
Dance and play in the green dripping dew
But deep down inside, there's still a spring tide
In the life that I still share with you.

ON PERSONAL AND POLITICAL HEALTH

You talk to your doctor
And within a few days
All his friends
Are inviting you out on dates.
Most are after your blood
Some are looking for consenting adults
To 'do things to'.
The ones who contacted me
Seemed particularly interested
In my backside and privates.
How could I resist
This new and exciting world?
I've now been contacted
By an elite group
Who might want to inject me
With nuclear fuel
Radiate me, and or,
Pump chemicals into me
Or just cut bits out.
They are all very caring
And say they are trying, as it were
To broaden my horizons
Help me to face up to myself
Preserve my already good health.

Then, there is Donald Trump, Kim Jong, Putin
And Islamic State
As well as leaders of so-called democracies
Who are determined to fight
To preserve our 'freedom'
By feeding gullible people on a diet

Of extreme religious fundamentalism
Or porn and brutality
Fat and sugar
And the banality of celeb-culture.

For the overriding imperative
Is that life can only get better
If our economy can be made to keep growing
At the expense of
The fish, birds, mammals and pollinators.

Some, of course, would simply
Kill all those who disagree with them
Because they are convinced
God wills it
Because He has chosen them
To purify the planet.

I am an organism
I was born and I shall die
I shall leave exactly the same
As Donald Trump
And the man selling The Big Issue -
But I am really truly grateful
For the interest shown in me
By my doctors;
They are in the main
My true friends, lovers and fellow human 'e' beings
i.e. they're not bullshitting politico/religio
Would-be saviours.

THE GOODBYE MAN

An armchair and a thin grey man:
A universe of spectral dreams;
He fought the battles of his time
And now sits musing in the streams
Of love and hate and hope and fear,
Of now and when and how and why –
He does not criticize so much
But contemplates the newsprint now –
The weave, the warp, the hidden side,
His life within the maze of thread;
He looks back from the mountain top,
I see that look - and softly tread
On past him to an empty chair,
Take up my paper – spread my wings
Around the world – the page is bare...
Drum – empty of enduring things!
I glance across – he knows I see
And smiles a last goodbye to me

LOSERS AND LOVERS

Metro-man in the middle lane
With tabloid mind and A4 brain
Still-born, snail-safe statistician.
Life's deadening drone
Predictable, derisible,
Respectable, forgettable,
Bureaucratic clone:
Sighs a last petition,
Loves alone.

Desperate artist sucks life's tit,
Hungrily drains each drop of it;
Drunken, spawns a new creation,
Life's poor weeping wit,
So ostentatiously conscious,
So dangerously contagious,
Memorable shit
Final shout of freedom,
Life's love lit.

SHALLOW

It is easy to fool bin-brains
Give moth-minds a light to buzz around
Twittering and tweeting
Drawn to comment on any trivial or deeper event
Propagandised on screen
In tabloid simplicity
Or 'intellectualised' in a broad-sheet's semi-seriousness.

Quisling governments pander to transnational interests
And call them national responsibilities
But worse
Dress them in ethical clothes –

So take a picture of a shot child
Clinging to its dead mother
In that country where there are transnational interests
And lo – war is justified!
While in neighbouring states
Hundreds, peacefully protesting, are shot.
But these would-be democrats
May not share, or even acknowledge
Transnational interests.
So let them die as doomed idealists
But file a token report -
A small, unimportant, blood-letting story
Between news of Jordan's new breast implants
And the latest winner of the European Lottery.

For blood is not as thick as oil –
It has no power to grease the grinding cogs
Of economic growth
Or the palms of grasping, monkey politicians.

THE IDOL OF TIME

Why is it that we measure out
Our lives against our ticking clocks
The seasons come, the seasons go
And play upon the weathering rocks

The light- years of the fleeing stars
The spectrum of their radiation
We think reveals the Bang and Birth
The linear path of our creation

The Greenwich line, atomic clock
Our yardsticks measuring the flow
Of myriads strokes on one small string
A fixed point on the moving bow

Yet time to flea or elephant
Bird or fish or wayside flower
Is not a metronomic beat
Of sixty seconds to the hour

We honour calculating brains
Objectifying time and motion
Vivisecting time and matter
Schizoid in their cold devotion

Yet on our own event horizon
Immeasurable round each Black Hole
Exuding into new dimensions,
Timeless to the inner soul

Sing quanta strings of dancing life
Elysian fields of sound and light
Winging in and out of matter
Without a measurement in sight

WARNING

When you have analysed this sod
Revolving round it's blistering sun
Decoded every genome's string
You'll still be carrying a gun.

You guard the frontiers of your soul
But angry fears, imprisoned deep
Betray the image you project
And test the sentries of your sleep.

And wakening, looking down the track
You'll still think you're a rational man
And more so, as mass fear and hate
Explode from out the festering can.

When every screen is filled with blood
And every street is fortified –
Will your integrity survive
Outside the limits of it's pride.

Will you then seek to serve a saviour
Some charismatic politician
Who'll fight to save what you are losing
Disguised within your own tradition?

Who'll blame your fears on all who're different
Tempting you to take his bait
Rebuild the Britain we have squandered
And march with him to purge the state.

If you join him, you will betray
Columba, Patrick, Aidan's way
When heathen hordes thought might was right
And tried extinguishing the light.

'YOU CAN BE AS GODS'

Transcendent love is banished.
The laboratory of earth
Lies prostrate 'neath man's scalpel
Assayed for what it's worth.

Re-engineer productive genes
Inject them into beast and seed
Ignorant, as your leperous hand
Disturbs the genome of each breed.

That's learnt to dance to it's own tune
To freely sing within the whole
Harmonic, earthly orchestra –
But you would play another role.

That of tone-deaf, blind transcriber
Creator of the super weed
Hear the alien pollens growling
In tuneless, terminator seed.

You petty gods, dissecting life
To profit from the copyright
Of genes you've changed in rice and maize –
The hungry farmers' sole birth right.

You experts of the single twig
Unconnected to the bough
Let alone the trunk and roots
Sacrificing all – for now.

THE HEART HAS IT'S REASONS
WHICH THE REASON CANNOT KNOW
(French proverb)

Counting and measuring
The micro and macro
Of time and space
Seeking to reach consensus
With reasoning brains
That continually differentiate
In their subjective experience of reality -
Subjugating individuality
To build a modern babel tower
From whose rising turret
Some day, the universe will be stripped bare
And it's latent function and powers
Be understood and harnessed.

'And the gods laugh'

For what we see is but an excrusion
Of semi-conscious knowing
A resonation of frequencies of light and sound
In three dimensions of dancing matter
Which the physical organ of the brain
Vainly attempts to comprehend
And interpret
It's experience to itself,
It's environment and destiny.
And yet this brave light of science
Shines in the darkness
To reveal multi-dimensions
Of timeless, vibrating frequencies

Holding these traumatised, ravaged three
Together.

Yet the technologists 'comprehended it not'
For the great majority chose to believe
In number and measure,
Clinging to tangibles
Brain-focused and analytical
Rather than spirit-centred
Fooling themselves that the whole
Will be revealed by the dissection of it's parts
That observation of an infinitesimal particle
Winging in and out of matter
Will reveal the pattern of the great dance.

Only a black hole awaits
To swallow the named part
That blinks enticingly
On the event horizon –
While in the world of matter,
The stressed, self-conscious brain
Having divorced itself from unbounded consciousness
Can only observe
The veiled, whirling dance-
Too proud to participate
In such simple, childish antics.

'He whom the gods would destroy
They first make mad'.

For the technologies derived from the sciences
Are used solely to build a global consumer empire
That exploits and desecrates the very eco-systems
Of which humankind is but a part
And on which it is wholly dependent.

A new, anthropocentric religion has been formulated
In which man is the figurehead
On time's ship rocketing toward the stars.
Shaped by naked, brute endeavour
He emerged from a primaeval soup
To conquer the vicissitudes of nature
And 'became as gods'.

In the light of this religion
All others are seen as mere fear-centred superstitions
Keeping men from seizing
'The knowledge of the tree of good and evil.'

This religion dismisses the intuitive knowing
Of holistic, eternal consciousness
And sets up a clockwork empire
In the three tangible dimensions of space and time,
Based on knowledge and observation of the world today.
It needs time, like a junkie needs heroin
Firstly, to organise itself more and more efficiently
And secondly, to establish it's continuity.

But any dating system must be based on a constant
Or knowledge of how long a natural process may take –
Such as radio-carbon dating.
But is the radiation hitting the earth today
And absorbed by all that is alive,
The same quanta of radiation
Absorbed by living things 10,000 years ago?
If the thickness of the atmosphere was not the same
(E.g. if weakened by the impact of a comet or volcanic eruption)
The dates would be different.
Was the ice-age a sudden cataclysmic event
Or slow evolutionary process?
Sedimentary rock is measured by the number of layers laid down.

Is this always a slow, gradual process,
Or can such a rock be formed in a few short years –
As has been observed after the Mount St Helen's eruption?
Can even a relatively modern artefact always be dated accurately?
Samples of the Turin Shroud
Analysed by secular scientists
Give a 14th Century date
While some catholic scientists, equally qualified
Have dated it at 2,000 years old.

We see what we want to see
And final objectivity eludes us.
This applies as much to the religious
As to the secular scientist,
Whose evolutionary orthodoxy
Often pre-determines their narrative of pre-history –
Because it assumes that
Geological, climatic and cosmic forces
Were the same thousands of years ago
As they are today,
That spiritual and psychological states of being
Were the same then as now.

All changes, as the dance unfolds
And there are no fixed points
At the quantum level of reality
That subtends and holds our three, temporal dimensions together.
The scenery and backdrop
Are changing constantly
Sometimes slowly, sometimes dramatically.
And we adapt epi-genetically
To our enfolding part in the play.

It is not our smallness we are afraid of
It is our potential greater depths

And it is our trust in technologies
To re-shape our planet in our own small image
That brings increasing disaster and disease
Upon us and the rest of creation.

Yet we are all far deeper and bigger than we know.
Only by returning to the ground of our being
And bathing in it's nutrient – filled springs
Can we begin to find wholeness and healing
And true knowing.

MILLENIUM

A window of wonder
Creaked open – briefly
Some looked up
Probing the glittering heavens
The alien spaces,
Hoping against hope
To see angels
Or at least some imprint
Of transcending personhood –
Some small indication
That we shall not have to
Bear ourselves alone
Through another thousand years
Self – making
New, distraught futures.
But we only saw
Reflections of ourselves,
Vast expanses of emptiness,
Pin-pricked patterns
Of star signs
Revolving around us
Evoking long lost nightmares
Of mad meteorites
Shattering our egg-shell world
And it's small, rigid orthodoxies –
Like a crazed gunman
In a school playground.

Yet love,
Pressing down time's tunnel
Light – imprinting the inner landscape
With living myth

Exhaled a dream
Of Eden
From which we,
Mad apes
Cast ourselves out to
Stab our way up
Through a vortex
Of loneliness
Towards a polluted trough
A single, sterile chalice.

One rock from the heavens,
One shudder from the earth,
One viral drink from a carcass we have killed,
And we shall be no more
Than a curse
To those who survive.

Too late, too late
We worship time
And are ignorant of it –
All the multi-varied tempos
Singing to make the planet sweet.
We savage the dark
With artificial light
But are more afraid of light and dark
Then ever before.
We can no longer really see
Really hear
Really sing
Really play.
We prefer processed husks to a natural feast,
Drugs to a dance,
Information to communication,
Images to reality

THE LEAKING RAFT OF REASON

Today, most live upon the surface
Trying not to drown,
While secular science,
Hubristic in the comforting delusion of progress
Surveys the bankless stream from it's leaking raft
Denying the insights of it's greatest seers
Who continue to challenge their lies
Of objectivity and linear time.
These neo-Darwinian fundamentalists
Have made a ragged raft of reason
A gim-crack nest of twigs and branches
On which they perch
Ignoring – vilifying the eternal quantum currents,
The whole dancing movement of life and matter
Dream-lapping and sweating
Through the brittle mortar of their intellectual dogmas.

Like their enemies, the creationists
They worship time
Measuring it out by light-year and nano-second
Until the mathematical formulae lose all emotional
correspondence
With even their own three-dimensional thinking;
After all, if you restrict yourself to three dimensions
Yet believe there may be at least eleven
That have some inter-reaction with this sensual triad,
Knowing that the brain's capacity for data analysis
Incapacitates itself
Through it's delusional belief in complete objectivity –
You can only freeze-frame small parts of the living picture
Analysing the bits

You have chosen to observe and examine –
As you drift downstream
Upon your leaking raft.

Like the creationists they believe in omnipresence –
For they have knowledge of the photon and electron,
Which are everywhere and at once
That everything is photonic/electronic
Nothing is separate.

They become mad through disassociation
Magnifying their own worth within the whole
Refusing to learn the simple dance steps
Of dynamic love.

THE SOMME AND AFTER

The very springs of life compressed
Culverted along timed, rigid, day lengths
Yet aching for a glorious life
Of uncharted freedom.

The drums begin to beat
The bugles sound
Awakening the sleeping power
Of legend and myth
Calling, calling,
Would-be warriors to rally round
A re-washed, bloodied flag again.

Once more the patriot cards are played
The king and knave of hearts
That youthful prince
That embodiment of willing sacrifice.
Yet neither he nor his father will lead
For they are now but symbols
Manifestations of the nations' pomp and pride.
No – let those who fought
The Mahdi and the Boer
Re-fight their wars
Re-visit the battle plans
Of past victories and 'victorious withdrawals'.
Let these loyal, be-medalled ignorant –
Vain believers in empire and racial superiority
Dance to the music
Composed by industrialists and bankers
The real lords of the land.

'Fog shrouds my mind
And the enemy in front
I wait as I have always waited
For a way to open up
Freeing my tight-coiled soul
From this self-dug graven trench –
While our overwhelming canon
Shell-scream at the Hun
Pulverising their wire and weapons
Blasting gaping holes through their defences
For endless days and nights.'

'Our generals know.'

'At last the bugles and the whistles blow
Uncoiling, we climb out and
Walk
Towards our enemy
For we are told we do not need to
Run
Eviscerating tracer
Leaden hail-storm.

'Who raised our flag?
This bloody, simple, symbol
In front of sacrificial pawns
Like me?'

'The children of the dead
We left behind
Will grieve throughout their lives
And to assuage that awful angry ache
Seek to emulate
And prove themselves as warriors.'

'Some of us survived
And while ostensibly alive
Were now in purgatory
Re-living over and over
The ever-present traumas
The horrors that can never, ever
Be explained or understood
Yet always conscious of a
Spring
That sprang too soon
And withered before it's semi-orphaned children
Who, creeping fearfully around
Our silent spectres
Now dance away – further and further
From hearts too stunned
To hold and re-assure them
Too locked-in
To let the sunshine through.'

'Live while you can
Before the madness
Overtakes the world again
And the drums beat
And the bugles blow
And the bombs and shells
And storms of lead
Shred the lives
Of your own generation.
Dance away – away – away
And let me go.'

DUNBLANE

I sold four guns in sweet Dunblane
To a lonely man with an angry brain,
I knew him well, he kept the law
'For sport,' he said, and I closed my door.

I sold guns to Saddam Hussein
A lonely man with an angry brain,
I knew him well, he was at war
'For peace,' he said, and I closed my door.

Sixteen infants – the man's insane!
I knew every one: I'm not to blame.
Laid my wrath on the red gym floor,
And wrung my hands, then closed my door.

Guns secure jobs, and foreign pain
Is not like it is in sweet Dunblane,
Gun exports are approved by law,
'Cause five thousand Kurds don't live next door.

OH GOD! REFLECTIONS ON 9/11 AND AFTER

From Al-qaeda to Isis

'See how we've fire-bombed your temples Great Satan
Your money-towers pointing at God
Armageddon has come to your proud Pentagon.
First strikes of the Holy One's Rod'.

'Al – qaeda believe this world's evil
Man must keep his flesh pure in death's gate
To enjoy paradise with the houris
Eat the choicest of food from God's plate.

'This world's a bleak desert, relentless and cruel
Through the curse of Eden's closed door
Though every oasis a symbolic crasis
A sign of the new heavenly shore.'

'Clean is the mind in a desert with God – foul
The city where God is cast out.
The desert makes pure all true hearts that endure
Like swords hammered free of all doubt'.

The president believes – God being absent,
America is His chosen clan
God wants us to strain to develop our brain
To genetically improve his plan.

'We'll re-engineer nature and our natures too
For that is our God-given right.
We've cast off the skin of original sin
For we're redeemed Children of Light.'

'And we shall create our own star – our own fate
In gold, or of bitter-sweet myrrh
No room at our table for those from a stable
No space for a mad crucifer.'

Down by the rivers, the Tigris, Euphrates
Where Eden was born in the mind
Fire rains from the sky on new altars raised high
To the dead, the maimed and the blind.

'We're God's chosen surgeon to abort your sick seed
From your womb-bunker deep underground
Where infantile fury craves Allah's glory
And curses what it's never found'.

'Oh rise up Muslim brothers, oh rise up and fight
A Jihad to free our unborn
Smash this Christian crusade, fire the Zionist stockade
Come die for a fear we can't mourn'.

'Hurl yourself at the earth and set it ablaze
Kill your heart by the word in your head
Allah's frustration with his own creation
Demands blood, yet more blood to be shed.'

'And whether that blood be from Shia or Sikh,
Or Atheist, Christian or Jew
So long as you kill for the sake of His will
The glory will all be to you.'

And now from that wasteland, that womb that was Eden
Where exiled souls hunger for home
They're rebuilding Babel with a USA label
Re-using the same scattered stone.

Where the scorpions are hiding and lying in wait
To strike at their conqueror's hand

Til the burden of loss cries out from their cross
'Bring back our boys from that god-empty land.'

'With a bomb round my belly midst those that I hate
Or driving a semtex filled car
I will hold to my lie that your world has to die
Destroyed by my own abattoir.'

'Oh, why do I burn for the Eve that I spurn
Evil temptress who sets me on fire
I must shroud her in black, so if I look back
I'll not see my true heart's desire.'

'For I'll only be blessed to lie on her breast
Forever – a martyr on high
If I fight for the state of the true Caliphate
And always be willing to die.'

'We are as sharp as the flail of a sandstorm
Your cities, soft-naked as whores
In London and Bali, Mumbai, Nairobi
You've now felt the power of our cause.'

'Yes in Manchester, in New York, and Brussels
With knives or a truck or a car
You'll never know when we'll strike you again
In a market or concert or bar.'

'For you've kicked over the fire and scattered
Embers to set martyrs aflame
Now you've nowhere to hide, for we are inside
To bomb you and shoot you and maim.'

'Did you hear what we said as you buried your dead
When we bombed you in Paris and Spain
We said 'you worship life, while we honour death'
This death that you fear is our gain.'

'Which is why you can't win, though the power of your sin
Forges arms the world's never seen.
Yet we've put you in jail, inside your chainmail
Trapped, cowered by the blood of the clean'.

'You ask why we believe and act as we do
And how we have come by our Name?
Our fruit was rejected, your slain lamb accepted
Yes – we are the Children of Cain!'

Now drones sweep the skies like falcons
Quartering the land for their prey
Controlled from a screen, by soldiers unseen
Absorbed in a safe video play.

Ancient hatred like flesh-eating cancers
Consume Sunni and Shite and Jew
Protestant, Catholic, Communist, Atheist
Capitalist, Buddhist, Hindu.

Dare we waken the man from his slumber
Kill the tyrant who keeps him asleep
For at the sound of reveille, his demons will rally
And a wolf explode from the sheep.

....

See Abraham's offspring, pilgrims and strangers
Alone on the wild Milky Way
Hungry the heart-long for echoes of star-song
Each absorbed in their own Passion Play.

There in the mosque, submitting to Allah
In the Church remembering the Cross
In the Synagogue, reading the Torah
Competing hot-lines linked straight to one Boss.

Each convinced God's recorded one message –
You'll recognise His voice by the tone
But you'll only get through, if you're born a Jew
Or use a Christian or Muslim cell-phone.

Yet all agree God is One, Just and Holy
A Spirit of compassion and grace –
So why this selection, the ego's projection
Of these 'bit-gods' in human mind-space?

Could it be that they've got God's old number
Or when they call, it's inopportune?
But when I phoned God, his reply was quite odd
'I am there when you're here – catch you soon'

And did I dream that I saw a man walking
As soft-quiet as the breeze moves the air
With a spirit so raw,that only a whore
Stooped to bind his sore feet with her hair?

UNBORN

When your blank boot
Smashed into that defenceless face
Again and again
A face you'd never met before
Eyes you'd never looked into –
You revealed your real terror
Of becoming human(e)
Your terror of feeling joy
Your terror of love.
That's why you hate your own soul
That's why it is so malformed
So furious in it's feeling of impotence
So hopeless.
Did your own father hate you,
Your mother ignore you
That you displayed such little humanity?
Has there ever been anyone in your life
Who cherished you
Such that it challenged your cowardice?

Every child seeks love
But now you have reached the chronological age of adulthood
You have stopped looking for it
And chosen only to hate anyone and everything
That has the courage to grow in gentleness.

LIVING THE IMAGE
(Reflections on the film 'Spring Breakers')

They screen out
All the smells and sweat
All the wild, barbarian growth
Springing from the rampant earth
Their living, breathing mother.

Earphones executing songs
Drumming rain and choralling lark
Alone – web-bound they shout for hearing
Publicise their outward worth
Compare the image of each other.

The being's arid seed cries out
To root and shoot and flower and fruit
To give and meet, and spread it's seed –
But all it hears are tombstone texts
Terse, brain-tweets of a robot lover.

Sell the image of your body
Kiss your unformed soul goodbye
Fulfil each siren ad-man's message
To keep the ego's flame alive.
There is no book beneath the cover.

IN THE MOUNTAINS

We have come to your wilderness
For healing
For we are sick of accountants' analysis
And the tensions of tabloid terrors.
Within your ancient, oh so ancient
Dumb stillness
We recognise our deepest need
And cling like heather
To your bosomed slopes
Rooting ourselves
Into your waiting skin –

While in the valley
Unconscious men drive blinkered on
Counting the units
Of their measured roads.

IN AND OUT

I've traversed the borders of madness
In four dimensions of dance
Probed the horizons of Kismet
And suckled the memory of chance.

But the quanta have kept all their secrets
Forced me back into their play
Of simple, organic-becoming
In the three dimensions of clay.

WIND

The wind blew open my heart's door
I cursed, and slammed it shut once more.
I cried atop a ravaged hill
Till only silence made me still.
And in that silence grew a voice –
Victim or victor was my choice.

ELIZABETHANS
(Boot Hill is the highest point of Northam near Bideford in Devon)

The church tower – a blunt digit
Atop Boot Hill
Thrust upwards into the dancing cosmos
A memorial to the permanent impermanence
To all the timed lives
Homed around.
Their graves breathe out moss covered memories
Decade after decade
Century after century
To each succeeding generation
And - since industrial times,
Believing in their own betterment.

Those focussed on the chancel ritual today
Would flee their sacred building
If those in the earliest graves
Were resurrected
And marched into Sunday worship -
If first Elizabethans suddenly intruded
Into second Elizabethan times
Oh yes, they would not just flee
From such a frightening phenomenon
They would flee
From the strength and coarseness of their language
Their physical directness and robust condemnation
Their preoccupation with hell
Their Shakespearian lewdness.
Their superstitious 'madness'.

And what of these Tudor intruders?
What would they make of their religious bequest

To today's Elizabethan souls?
These weak bodies
So concerned with hygiene and being 'nice'
Repressing their passions beneath comforting ritual
And personal correctness
Reliant on technological prowess and innovation
Confusing communication with information exchange
Believing in everything and nothing.

Yet if they were given the time
To let the deep heart's silent witness
Breathe it's wisdom
Through the brain's mad groaning
Each generation would say
Their life had just begun
As they relaxed into the light
They had all been born from.

LINDY LOU

I will be the ground in which you grow
As I will grow in yours;
The laughter tumbling round your tight defended bud
That once cringed before the frost's accusing finger
Freezing your growth.
I will bring the spring rain
And the warm breeze that sings the songs of hope
Not the arctic gales
That made your tendril blooms cower
And run from rock to rock
Hiding
They shall blow no more from that quarter
And I will be your wind-shield from any other.
Then grow and bloom
And meet me on this timeless plain
And let us dance awhile
Together.

THE SCORE

She told me she'd scored
Last night
But underneath
She looked scarred
And her need was so acute
It pierced my senses
Demonly desperate
Helplessly homeless
Aching for acceptance
Running on empty
She'd not yet hit twenty.
Once again
The bull had scored.

HEART TIME/BRAIN TIME

The time of the heart
Is not
The time of the brain
That plans, assesses, weighs the future
Lives in conclusions.
The heart grows without planning
According to it's own
Reasonableness
In it's own
Timeless
Inconclusive way –
An organism
Not
A mechanism.

LOOKING FOR COMPLETENESS

Sex – brief assurance of meeting
As love seeks a meeting of mind
Flickering flame in the storm wind
Crying for the twin of it's kind.

Mind – distillation of spirit
Expressing the sense of the whole
Loving the dance of the moment
The passionate meeting of soul.

LAST PETAL

Only the mad – the dumb dreamers
Heard
The last pink petal sigh
On her fragile fluttering
Downward – deadward.
Even they
Did not see, did not reach,
Try to pluck
The wounded flower
From my thornless stem;
Take my sacrifice
And press its fading colour-warmth
Against another's breast.

This maimed mutation,
Irradiated – too weak to grasp
Is become a useless weakling
In a bee-less world.
Better the roar of neutered power,
The mega-tonnage,
The megabytes,
The sterile concrete –
Than the prophetic silence,
The softening pain
Of a falling petal.

BIOCIDE

Alfresco – a spread of sweating honey and jams
Elderflower champagne bubble-lipping a glass.
The sun, dapple-dancing through the laden apple tree
Leaves digesting the light.
The swooping charisma of a kingfisher
Dazzles the deeper pools of a mind-easing brook.
A hedgerow, bosomed with berries aching to be eaten
Shades a dozing hedgehog
And a grass snake sunbathing by a heated stone,
But only an occasional bee-murmur
And a smaller choir of birds –
Not the massed voices that once were heard
Treble-trembling the air
When the wild was wanton in it's guiltless enjoyment
Of surging sperm and sap.
You cannot remember –
Those battalions of butterflies waltzing among the flowers,
Dragonflies skate-dancing over the water
On a lazy July afternoon?

Fewer worms work the soil that is no longer fed,
The bee, wasp and moth work the blossom and flowers,
But we only hear our own busy industry – not theirs,
So come to believe their diminishing silence is normal –
These health workers of our own nutrition
And the hosts of other termites and insects.
But we are now time-lords,
Callous, ignorant masters of the planet
Existing on a self-made web of atomised information
Carelessly polluting the atmosphere
With molecules of insecticide and pesticide

To maintain our own anthropocentric, imperial power.
And those hosts of little, buzzing fluttering creatures?
Collateral damage of our self-deluding war on nature.
Biocide is suicide.

BREAKING FREE

I found a grave atop a mountain
Dug beneath a cairn of stone
And on a slate I saw was written
'This is not my real home'.

'Do not cling to flesh and tissue
Do not grieve for bones and blood
Do not pine for brain and sinew
The worms will turn them all to mud'.

'But sing of that enlivening spirit
The light intelligent inside
Creating springs of living quanta
Upon an island in life's tide'.

'Until was formed a conscious person
Who fearfully learnt to be humane
Who faltering, danced in three dimensions
And slowly learnt his real name –

Which is the one you might remember
If you have loved what must survive
This chrysalis beneath this cairn-pile –
This butterfly is more alive'.

QUESTIONS I CANNOT ANSWER

'Tell me the time; please tell me the time'
Soft-questioned my own trusting child.
'How long will the earth swing round the sun
Before there're no lions in the wild?'

'Will the ozone layer disappear?
Will the plants all wither and die?
Will we be able to sledge again
As the earth gets hotter and dry?'

'Will I see playful dolphins and whales,
And will there be fish in the sea?
Will there be jungles when I grow up
That I will be able to see?'

'Will elephants, tigers and hippo
Still be roaming the lands they knew?
Or will they be fenced in like prisoners,
Look as sad as those in the zoo?'

'Will there be streets where I can still play
Safely without being molested?
You've watched tv; will you play with me
In the garden, now you've rested?'

I didn't reply, but got to my feet,
No excuses, I'm on the 'dole'.
And I knew as his small hand clasped mine,
It was me he tried to console.

TOWARDS THE KINGDOM

Outside, the snow lay like a shroud
Death's drape upon the waiting earth
Inside, I let the silence drain
My ego's analysing worth

The atmosphere was warm and kind
With fire- warmth breathing from the grate
Red wine to stimulate and soothe
My passage through the listening gate

And waiting, waiting with sweet love
The king drew back my shaking veil
And planted kisses of deep now
Upon the head that sought his grail

BE STILL

Shall I worship at your altar
Try placate your ancient fears –
Or seize the fluttering offering
And launder it with tears.

But I believe beyond religion
Still voice inside the trembling quake
The real you, born deep in fear
With fiendish nightmares lurking there
Which love may yet awake.

TIME AND THE TIMELESS

In the timeless ground of being
The living water
Swimming with nutrient thought
Picture-filled ideas
Rises up the spine
Through the semi-conscious limbs
To spark the synapses
Of the brain
And express a new creation

In the time-slicing, exiled world
Where every hour is counted
Every minute chased
In the race to squeeze a second
Off another competitor,
The fevered brain
Analyses, assesses
Computes it's options
Shielding it's inner eye
While picking from the torrent of information
Rushing by.

The spine curves towards the screen
The heart wilts in the spiritual drought.

The self-defending person
Has nothing new to say
Nothing new to express.
Asleep – it is disturbed
Awake – it strains to survive
Keep it's senses alert
Blindly seeking communion
Through an exchange of images
Before it falls back
Into the dark.

Ah – if it had only trusted,
Stopped spectating,
Thrown itself from the mythical bank
Into the stream
Where the springs of the untimed world
Of the quantum plane
Lap at the citadels of illusion
Ever creating,
Renewing the life of the world
From the boundless kingdom within
Calling the life-lonely spirit
To dance with the eternal.

A SPELL TOO EASILY BROKEN

Say nothing
When the light-silence
Transfigures the hills
Or shrouds them in rain
Say nothing
When the light-silence
Climaxes in dawn
Or relaxes in setting
Let the communion of the transcendent dance
Be our shared un-utterance
No movement, no comment
Above all
No asking
If the knowing
Was mutual
If this trans-substantiation
Of common elements
Has really co-joined us
In its rapturous communion.

SONGS

MOVE ON

Move on, climb your mountain
Move on, find your dream
We'll meet again some new morning
Tell each other what we've seen

Move on, your bud must open
Feel the wind, the frost and rain
Move on, your life is waiting
Move on, and find your name

Move on, don't look behind you
Move on, don't feel ashamed
You can stand upon my shoulders
Never want to see you tamed

Move on, find your meaning
You can't live within my shade
Move on, new friends are waiting
Move on, don't be afraid

Move on, your anchor's straining
Haul it up, catch the tide
Plot a course and set your sails now
I'll see you on the other side

Trust the guiding star within you
Let is shine for all to see
In sun or mist of stormy weather
Grow in your integrity.

THE BANKER'S SONG
(to the tune of The Moonshiner)

I'm a banker, I'm a gambler
Without any care
I'll conjure your money
Make it all disappear
If I win I make millions
If I lose I make more
I'm the slickest of spivs
On the whole trading floor.

I gamble with hedge funds
Derivatives too
Where it all goes to
I haven't a clue
I really don't care
'Cause I've got my cut
In a safe tax-free haven
Where the bars never shut.

We'll launder your money
Just make us a pitch
Dictator or drug lord
Or just super-rich
We've mis-sold insurance
And rigged interest rates
If you're poor we will screw you
If you're rich we're your mates.

We've top civil servants
MPs on our books
Republican leaders
Accountants and crooks

They avoid paying taxes
Their wealth is offshore
'Cause that's what a UK
Tax haven is for.

We kept selling debt
Like dud packets of three
To sailors on shore leave
Soon returning to sea.
Well, the tide always flows
And the tide always ebbs
And the losers as ever
Are the credulous plebs.

They gave me a title
When I put 10k down
Then 50k more
Bought a nice ermine gown
The party was grateful
In awe of my skill
For conjuring wealth
From statistical swill.

The credit crunch's come
But it don't bother me
I still got my bonus
Plus a good severance fee
Now I'm advising
The inept FCA
For one day a week
And 65k

(Repeat verse 1)

JERUSALEM – Betrayed!
(To the tune of Jerusalem)

And shall these drills in modern times
Frack through the fields of England green
And shall those towers of slashing blades
On every hill and mount be seen
And shall her birds and bees and moths
Her badgers, trees and butterflies
Expire in this polluted air
Struggling beneath the empty sky

And shall we watch as nuclear waste
Poisons her rivers, brooks and seas
And ancient woods are chain-sawed down
While market men do what they please
And vast estates o'er come the land
To cage the screen-attentive throng
And GM weeds discord the tunes
Of England's children's shattered song.

Tell me the worth of an English wood
The cost of a nightingale's sweet song
The market price of eagles' eggs
Whether owls and robins still belong
Any more in this your barren land
Where now a withering hand holds sway
And freedom's wind and freedom's sky
Strain at their shackles every day.

Chorus:
Bring me my bow etc

RICH FOOL
(To the tune of 'I am Sailing')

I am building
I am building
On the greenfields
By the sea
And I'm banking
Loads of money
Loads of money
Just for me.

I am richer
So much richer
Than all the losers
Poorer than me
Their just thicker
I'm much slicker
Feeding off them
Like a flea.

Greed's my armour
Greed's my drama
My role defending
The real me
'Cause I dare not
Let my soul out
Risk my love's true
Liberty.

But I'm lonely
Oh so lonely
In my penthouse
With Porsche and pool
Death draws nearer
Where's the carer
That truly loves this
Poor greedy fool?

BALLAD OF THE FIGHTING FARMER
(to the tune of 'Dublin in The Green')

Chorus

We're all off to London in the Spring in the Spring
Our muck-spreaders stinking in the sun
And never will we hurry as we spray our slurry
From Westminster to Kensington.

I am an angry farmer
I milk and plough all day
But now my back's against the wall
May have to sell and move away.

But the farm's been in my family
For at least 200 years
In peace and war we've fed the poor
But now nobody cares.

We're strangled by the bureaucrats
And supermarkets too
And urban man doesn't give a damn
Unless we spoil his view.

MAFF approved new cattle feed
Then my herd got BSE
They heaped 'em in a pyre, and lit the bloody fire
And then they tried to blame me.

They closed my local abattoir
Now my farm's in quarantine
We've now got foot and mouth, and my income's headed south
'Cause my herd's been shot and with it's gone my dream.

A salesman came to me from a GM company
Said 'We'll pay you for your fields
Our terminator seed is just the thing you need
To increase your maize yields.

I looked him up and down he must have thought I was a clown
And he – like a hungry fox'
'You mean -until the day I die I'll always have to buy
All my seed from your company's stock.

And another came to me said 'Inject this BST
And watch your profits grow
With this new TB alarm we'll gas the badgers on your farm
And pay you to say I didn't know.

But I love this land it's all I know
Don't like to farm this way
I'd like to treat the land as my father did
But I can't make it pay.

If I could live on subsidies
Then I'd stop using sprays
But I think that I'd be manic before I got organic
And return to my father's ways.

Now the wildlife's growing silent
And my wife grows silent too
I've just caught tonsillitis and the cows have got mastitis
The contractors phoned to say he has the 'flu.

In your supermarket shops for two lamb chops
They'll charge at least four quid
But my six fat lambs in market today
Hardly raised a bid.

My milk quota's just fallen
And the water bill is due
The sheepdog's lost his wits, more mastitis in the tits
What can a farmer do?

MAFF made me use that sheep dip
I'm so depressed I'm fit to burst
If it wasn't for my wife I think I'd take my life
But I'll fight in London first.

Chorus

THE BALLAD OF THE MPS EXPENSES
(To the tune of – the Wild Rover)

I've been your MP for many a year
And I spent all your money, took every due care
But please re-elect me, now I've paid back some loot
I managed to fiddle before this dispute.

Chorus

And it's yeah, yeah, ever
Yeah, yeah, ever, more, more
For I'm your hog member
Your honourable whore.

I'll tell you my tale if you're willing to hear
I was born to find claret, malt whiskey – not beer
Like those commoners drink in their houses so small,
I've always believed I had a much higher call.

I served on the Council, but the perks were quite thin
Then my whelk stall went bankrupt, and my wife hit the gin.
I felt hopeless and angry, and vented my spleen
Then my party said 'this man is hungry and mean'.

In the hustings I beat the do-gooding has-beens
And was chosen to echo my party's machine
With my no–nonsense sound bites 'bout Europe and cuts
Plus some local concerns about unmarried sluts.

My income as MP is a mere 70k
But with claims for expenses, I can double my pay
A second home in London and a flat by the sea
All mortgages paid for by a kind Treasury.

A larger home beckoned the fatter I grew
As did my status – 'twas only my due.
So I switch my main residence round every year –
To suggest this is greedy is really a smear.

It's a family business, when all's said and done
So I claim for my wife as well as my son.
She is my secretary, he drives the car
When he's not running his London wine bar.

I soon reached the limit of all I could claim
But at the start of the tax year, re-submitted again.
My duck house was sinking, it would no longer float
So I claimed for a new one, fixed the leak in the moat.

Three plasma screen tellies, five i-pods and more
Plus a new granny flat and a new ballroom floor;
I don't think you realise how long it takes me
To claim these expenses, but I hope you now see.

So now I've been candid, I've held nothing back
I feel hurt and betrayed to be put on this rack.
It's all about Britain – it's not about me - - - -
So please re-elect me as your local MP.

THE DEVON DEVELOPER
(To the tune of – 'The Thrashing Machine')

Down in fair Devon a builder did dwell
He saw some green acres and his heart did swell
'That's four hundred houses and five million quid
When my friends on the council have backed up my bid.'

Chorus

'I'll have it, I'll have it, I'll have it my way
Most councillors worship the rich of the day
If I offer a hall and five starter homes too
They'll jump at my plan and nod it on through.'

'There's an A.O.N.B. and a triple S.I.
A rough country park that I'll offer to buy.
But they won't be bothered they'll do all they can
When I've wined them and dined them, they'll vote for my plan.'

'For there's only one mantra that they understand,
Money more money if they sell off the land
To raise all their salaries, pensions and perks
With a little bit over to spend on new works.'

It's not just more houses they're eager to see,
It's more and more tourists paying a fee
To park in their car parks and spend money free
When they fumed in the traffic jams down on the quay.'

'But it don't bother me, I've a villa in Spain,
Plus an old country rectory down a quiet lane
Near a friendly thatched pub where they serve a good meal
2 miles from my golf club where I can swing a good deal.'

'Now I'm in limbo, I think I am dead –
A rich councillor friend at my graveside just said
'How much did he leave then?' he asked of his mate
'Everything, everything – he left it too late'.

Final Chorus

'I had it, I had it, I had it my way
The planet is dying, my children will pay
I made loads of cash, people thought I was smart
I wish I had heeded the voice of my heart.'

ONE LAST WISH
(to the tune of 'Rosin the Beau')

When we've felled all the trees in the forests
And exhausted the oceans of fish
Released all the methane and carbon
We'll still think we've got one last wish.

Chorus 1

We'll be wishing our children weren't crying
And cursing our greed and our pride
For polluting and raping the planet
While we binged as earth struggled and died.

Come worship the Lords of the Markets
Where the strongest are trampling the weak
Where the greedy are honoured as heroes
Instead of the poor and the meek.

The trough is already half empty
As we're fighting to shove our snouts in
While behind us bewildered and starving
The masses can see they can't win.

Chorus 2

As their children walk miles for some kindling
Dig for water with a stick for a tool
While some are watering their golf course
Re-filling their new swimming pool.

You're only a god when you're human
Humane when you seek out the light
But a devil when you hide in darkness
For yours is the kingdom of night.

Chorus 1

And did I dream that I saw a man walking
As soft-quiet as the breeze moves the air
With a spirit so raw that only a whore
Stooped to bind his sore feet with her hair.

Chorus 3

It's the children who see this man walking
At their pace with time for each one
And they can't understand why their parents
Run a race that can never be won.

CONSULTANTS
(To the tune of – The Sloop John B)

Consultants all are we
Experts as you will see
Round all the councils we do go
Writing reports
On all of their thoughts
This is the best con
We've ever been on.

Chorus:

So hoist the consultancy fee
'Cos we're the best, don't you agree
Course you do
That's why you pay us so much
Do keep in touch
It's been good being a crutch
For you to depend on
And thank you so much

Whatever you want we will write
We know you're not very bright
So we'll fill the report with lots of pie charts and pics
And dense statistics
To disguise any tricks
In the appendices
Where no-one will look.

We won't be holding your hand
If ever the shit hits the fan
But at least you can say
We took their expert advice
And they seemed very nice

And we paid a good price
To confirm the direction
We wanted to go.

If you were'nt so naïve or inane
You wouldn't employ us again
But we've got all your cash and added it straight to our stash
And then changed our name –
And you've employed us again
Oh – this is the best con
We've ever been on.

LOCAL ELECTION
(To the tune of – 'in the town of Reno')

T'was in a town in Devon
In Spring election year
The time when politicians
Suddenly appear
With rosettes big as sunflowers
And a salesman's slick handshake
And pleading eyes just like my dog's
When he sees I'm eating cake

'Can I count on you to vote for me
In this election year?
I'm fighting for the policies
That you and I hold dear.
I listen to the people
So please get out and vote
I'm completely independent
Within my party's coat.'

'And just what are your policies?'
I tried to ask of him
' I'm just a straight plain talker
I don't believe in spin'.
'So just what are your policies?'
I questioned him in vain
'I listen to the people'
He informed me once again.

'You're on the Plan's Committee
I recognise your mug.
You dine out with developers
At the local country club.'

'What are you suggesting?'
He bared his teeth at me.
'Have your interests all been listed
In the Members' Registry?'

'You stood as independent
Last election time
And then became a Tory
Six months down the line.
At the heart of all your thinking
Is – what's in it for me.
Your just a willing lackey
Of local industry.'

'I'll tell you what I'm looking for
In my local Councillor.
A person with a vision,
Someone who will roar,
Who understands the forces
That shape our world today,
Who will fight to heal our planet
'Cos there's no other way.'

'Your vision is consuming
More and more and more
And raiding the resources
That nature holds in store
For every generation
Who'll ever live on earth –
You know the current cost of things
But not their real worth'.

'You're mad' he said 'You're mad' said he
' There goes my mobile phone'
I said 'I'll still remind you

You'll reap what you have sown'.
He said – ' You're an idealist
As green as green can be'
I said – 'I am a realist,
You'll die the same as me.'

'Our little world is finite
Seven billion live on earth
And half of them are starving
And seen of little worth.
They want the same as you have
And you say – they'll have their day
To gorge themselves like you do
And let their children pay.'

'You're mad' he said 'You're mad' said he
' There goes my mobile phone'
I said 'I'll still remind you
You'll reap what you have sown'.
He said – ' You're an idealist
As green as green can be'
I said – 'I am a realist,
You'll die the same as me.'

TWITTER, TWITTER, TWEET

There she was, just walking down the street
Thumbing text twitter, twitter text, text twitter tweet
Phone to ear like a clamp-pad on a bleed
Thumbing text twitter, text twitter, text twitter, tweet
She looked good, she looked the same
As information strafed her brain.

Before I knew she was twittering to me
Thumbing etc
I hate my hips; I need botox in my lips
Thumbing etc
She looked mad, she looked sad
Underneath she's not so bad

Sometime later I saw her in the street
Twitching, jerk jitter, jitter jerk with fidget flitter feet
As desperate as a lamb upon an empty teat
Mumbling text twitter, twitter text, a flapping sort of beat
Hands free, ear grown
All the way around her phone

Oh, oh, I've seen the new breed
An ad-man's puppet on information speed.

I want a free-range woman with a free-range mind
Living with the rhythms of the natural kind
Not a battery-house chick – like a fashion-house stick
Crying text, twitter, twitter text, twitter, twitter, tweet
But earthy – sexy
Natural – friendly.

Made in the USA
Middletown, DE
31 August 2017